THE SE

MW00990422

Illustrations and Explanations
for Study Clubs of the Order
of the Eastern Star

By

SARAH H. TERRY

Grand Secretary, Grand Chapter of the Order of the
Eastern Star, Kentucky
(1911–1941)

MACOY PUBLISHING AND MASONIC SUPPLY CO., INC.

Richmond, Virginia

Other books by Sarah H. Terry:

Brief History of the Eastern Star
Brochure of the Life of Rob Morris
My Altar of Dreams (poems)
Shining Through (poems)

Editor of the Eastern Star Column in
"Masonic Home Journal" (Kentucky) from 1911 to 1941

Copyright, 1963
Macoy Publishing & Masonic Supply Co., Inc.
Richmond, Virginia

ISBN-0-88053-322-6

Printed in the United States of America

CONTENTS

PUBLISHER'S FOREWORD
TO THE TENTH EDITION

~~~~~~

"And whosoever shall compel thee to go a mile, go with him twain." *Matthew* 5:41 (King James Version)

"And if anyone forces you to go one mile, go with him two miles." *Matthew* 5:41 (Revised Standard Version)

THE title of this book is a fitting memorial to the one who wrote it—Mrs. Sarah H. Terry, who, throughout her many years of service to the Order of the Eastern Star, never failed to willingly do that "extra bit of work" for her sisters in the Order. Truly, she was one of whom it can be said that she spent her life "going the second mile."

Mrs. Terry was born in Indiana and taught school many years in Indiana and Kentucky. She was a charter member of Clarkson Chapter No. 12 in Kentucky and served in every office of that Chapter. In the State Grand Chapter, she held the offices of Grand Ruth, Grand Marshal and Grand Associate Matron before being elected as Grand Matron in 1906. Her term expired in 1907 when she was elected Grand Treasurer, followed, in 1911, as Grand Secretary, which office she held until her death in 1941.

In addition to her many duties in her State Grand Chapter, she found time to have four children (one daughter, Mary Terry Sloan, now lives in Texas); serve on the Ritual Committee of the General Grand Chapter; write poems; contribute many articles to fraternal magazines and papers; edit the Eastern Star section of the "Masonic Home Journal" (Kentucky) from 1909 to her death in 1941; teach Sunday School for more than 50 years; publish *A Brief History of the Eastern Star, Brochure on the Life of Rob Morris,* two books of poems, *My Altar of Dreams* and *Shining Through.* In 1935, she brought out the first edition of *The Second Mile,* which has been read and studied by thousands.

Hers was a full and busy life and we are proud to now take over the publication of *The Second Mile* in the tenth edition. The substance matter is the same as written by Mrs. Terry. Only minor editorial and typographical corrections have been made and the book has been set in more readable type.

THE PUBLISHERS

1963

FOREWORD

~~~~~~

In offering these lectures to the Order of the Eastern Star, I make no apology. They are but gleanings from here and there, with many original ideas of my own.

I have just given sufficient facts to make the reader eager for further study, with a hope that some bright mind may delve deeper and find more hidden meanings and give to a hungry people more of what the Order really stands for.

The reason of failure of all ritualism is because they cling too much to dogma, or tabulation, rather than to the deeper mysteries, or the spiritual side. A close study, therefore, is commendable and well worthy of our time.

The demand of the hour is not the idea that a mere recitation of the ritual is all there is to the Order, but to know what this ritual really means, and to create a feeling for the beautiful teachings the ritual portrays to the mind of the investigator is essential. The symbolic meaning of the various lessons is beautiful and should be studied by all who are privileged to become members of the Order.

Fraternally thine,
SARAH H. TERRY,
Grand Secretary

1935

"Books, books, books—give me ever more books, for they are the caskets wherein we find the immortal expression of humanity—words, the only things that live forever."

—Eugene Field.

INITIATION

~~~~~~

INITIATION means the getting of knowledge. All symbols we use are made up of straight lines or circles. The floor work is only a means, not an end. The symbols point to the light, which shows the individual the way.

In the study of symbolism, we should keep in mind that a symbol is but a figure of a truth, and that all symbols we use in the O. E. S. speak of the power behind the visible universe —the tremendous reality of the unseen.

The golden beams from the star, when rightly understood, should shine in our everyday life so much so that all the outside world may see the wonderful loyalty and friendship the members express for one another.

The Five Rays of the Star, when totaled, spell "SERVE." And that is our mission on earth—SERVICE. Our work is to proclaim the gospel of a Living Master and to prepare the world "TO SEE HIS STAR IN THE EAST."

SIGNS AND SYMBOLS

From the time God set His bow in the heavens to the end of the Sacred Record, there have been signs and symbols.

Since God spoke to Moses from the burning bush, gave to Gideon an understanding from the Fleece, to Elisha in the falling mantle, and to John the symbol of Baptism, He has directed mankind in His way by signs and symbols, and "only those who run may read."

Symbolism is the most ancient known method of imparting knowledge. It is much older than reading or writing. A symbol, or figure, of something intellectual or spiritual is a visible object representing to the mind the semblance of something which is not shown but realized.

The most ancient people used symbols to represent thoughts or words. The early man used those things which he saw about him as provided by nature—the growing things—the flowers and their colors, the trees, the rivers and waters. He studied these things to find a meaning of himself and the reasons for life, and from this study he formed certain conclusions to establish a system of symbols by which he handed down to posterity the knowledge he gained. Thus, we find pictured symbols on ancient stones, pyramids, and various walls of ancient buried cities in Persia, Babylon, Mesopotamia, Lydia, and other cities showing the dawn of development of man and his countries. Mexico has the pictured language of the Aztecs, America has the totem pole of the Indian, the language of which has been, in a way, deciphered by modern discoveries.

Finally, in the history of man and his country, these pictured words became syllables, then words, and finally developed into the phonetic alphabet, the world language.

Man still uses picture writing in its original form today when he wishes to attract attention. Advertisements are full of this primitive method. The dog listening for his master's voice in a talking machine tells a story in picture form. The Indian chief used this same method of recording a story when he drew a picture showing himself killing his enemy. In both cases the precise words are indicated; the idea comes directly, each observer putting in his own words.

Strictly speaking this was not writing at all for writing did not begin until some method was found for setting down definite words. But in words there is a certain form of symbolism—or hidden meaning, and in these pages we have tried to bring this meaning to the mind of the observer, according to our own interpretation.

It is always more interesting a little farther on, so I am asking you to go the second mile with me in our Eastern Star work.

You have ideas of your own. Use them as you study this book.

ADAH—*The Daughter*

~~~~~~

An Ornament　　　　　☆　　　　　GEM: *Turquoise*

RECORDED in the Book of Judges, written by Samuel, is the history of the Jewish Nation from Joshua to Samson.

Moses had been the lawgiver, judge and jury for all grievances among his people. This grew to be such a burdensome task that assistants were appointed to help in these deliberations. Joshua was the first Advisor in the Land of Promise, Moses having died before possession was made.

Then followed a series of leaders, called judges. The judges in conjunction with the prophets of their time, were both civic and spiritual lawgivers, and had access to the Oracles of the Lord, and interpretation of same through prophets and priests. There were thirteen judges.

Othneil, a near relative of Caleb, the great warrior and spy, was the first judge and under his leadership the people had rest for forty years. Then followed a system of judges of more or less valor, and among them we might mention Deborah, the woman who was chosen to go at the head of the army at one time. Outstanding also was Gideon and also Jephthah who was the ninth judge.

4

Adah—The Daughter

Jephthah was a resident of Gilead, having been banished when a young man, but he had never departed from the Jewish teachings and strictly maintained the Jewish faith as taught in the tabernacle each Sabbath. So firm was he in his faith and in the doctrinal belief in covenants that he stands in the Roll Call of Faith in Hebrews 11:32 as a martyr defender of truth.

The Promised Land—Canaan—was surrounded on all sides by tribes whose chief pleasure was warfare. Tribal wars caused no little trouble for the Jews during the conquest and, after they were established in the Promised Land, the victorious army gained or lost territory as they fought. Hence, every man was a warrior, and every woman loved his loyalty and bravery, and encouraged her loved ones for their valor.

Like Jacob of old, Jephthah was a bargainer and when his people called upon him, after a big defeat, to go at the head of the Army of Israel, he made provisions with the messenger, and then sacrificed unto the Lord making a vow that if He would give him the victory over the enemy he would offer as a burnt offering the first thing that came from the door of his house upon his return from Mispah in peace. Levitical law taught that to break a vow not only meant the forfeit of one's life, but it placed the one thus breaking in ridicule and all anathemas of Jewry would be heaped upon him. (Gen. 28:20–21; Num. 30:2)

The story of Jephthah, one of the judges, reveals the fact that human sacrifices were often made. There were two kinds of sacrifices, a Blood Sacrifice which meant the spilling of blood in the slaughter of beasts as the law demanded, and Burnt Offerings, told in Leviticus.

The second sacrifice was the putting aside, or separation for service in the Temple, or service of God mentioned in the Book of Samuel and more fully explained in Numbers 6—

5

which explains the Nazarite, or Devotee (or Devoted thing) something redeemed by payment of money, as told in Leviticus.

The lesson of Adah as given in the ritual beautifully illustrates Jephthah's determination to keep the vow he had made before assuming leadership of the army of the Lord. It leaves the impression that the daughter was slain according to the Levitical law (Lev. 1:1–6; 6:8–13).

Her father's heart, while broken, yet rejoiced in the keeping of his vow, and the bestowal of God's blessing upon him for the faith thus implied.

To be childless was a reproach among Jewish women, consequently the chief desire of all women was wedlock and children, in the hope that the promised Messiah might be born of one of them. Every maiden had a secret desire to become the mother of that promised Messiah.

Thus, we find that when acquainted with the vow made by her father, and remembering his integrity as a Leader of the people, and his faith in God, Adah asked that she be permitted to go to the mountains to prepare herself for death. This request was granted, and she and her maidens —and no doubt friends—bade her father a fond adieu to devote, in seclusion, a time to be used in the preparation for death.

If we take the story of the ritual we find that it carries out the blood sacrifice, and this lesson is given to teach us the binding force of a vow—the obligation we have just taken, and in maintenance of our Fidelity.

The prevailing style of dress for women of that period was a loose flowing robe with headdress resembling a scarf, or shawl, which covered the head, which could be drawn down over the face to protect the eyes from the blinding desert sun. Virgins never lifted the veil when in the presence of men.

Thus clad, this bevy of young girls returned from the mountains with hearts prepared to make any kind of sacrifice that would maintain the honor of Adah's father. He was found to be relenting, but spurred onto the deed of sacrifice as vowed to God, Jephthah was persuaded to perform a deed that made him famous throughout the annals of history.

The ritual story is clear in this act, and we only give here the fact that the loyalty of Adah to her father has not been excelled in all history. Her bravery, her willingness and her calm demeanor prove that it is not all of death to die, when that death is in the right.

The lesson to be learned is that our word should be our bond, our promises kept, our vows paid. How sacred we should hold our promises. How, above all, we should maintain our innocence through all trials of life, never forgetting that God is over all, and through all, and in all. We should trust His all-knowing Power, and keep our lives in conformity to His Divine will, so that, when the veil of mortality shall have been severed in twain, we may be prepared to clothe ourselves in immortality and go without fear into a willing death, having our eyes unveiled and fixed upon God and His throne.

The name "Adah" is not applied to Jephthah's daughter in the Bible story, but has been chosen for its meaning "Ornament." Jephthah's daughter was indeed an ornament to her race. There are, however, two other women mentioned in the Bible who bore the name Adah:

Adah, wife of Lamech—Genesis 4:19.
Adah, daughter of Elon—Genesis 36:2.
And in Second Kings we find Adiah.

VOWS—See Gen. 28:20-21, Numbers 30:2.
Judges 11:30.

THE SECOND MILE

Sign and emblem

In raising her veil, which was a mark of her virginity,
Adah proved not only her loyalty to her father, but the un-
mistakable right to die in full light of God's favor. Murderers
and mischief makers were led to the block blindfolded; she
was innocent and needed no such mask. Innocence marked
her life and stood by her in death. Obedience led her to the
Father's love and to her heavenly home.

The sword is typical of the right dividing God's laws, and
the principles of man. We are prepared to fight life's battles
only when we have our eyes unveiled to the face of God's
light. We are properly prepared for life's battles when we
wield the "sword of the Spirit" in defense of Christian virtues
of patience, meekness, long suffering, forbearance, and charity to all, separating the false from the true, the good from the
evil.

The veil is the covering, the earthly temple, the prison
house of the soul, which keeps us from attaining grander
heights. In life, the faithful seed must put off the veil of
matter that it may behold the beauty and wisdom of its
Creator, and thus Adah signifies spiritual illumination.

As a veil separated the Holy from the Most Holy place
in the Temple of Solomon, it is necessary after the sacred
obligation to have the veil lifted before the most holy virtues
be revealed by the Star Points. Hence, Adah's veil becomes
the symbol of Revelation.

Color

The color symbolic of this degree is typical of the blue
skies that overshadowed the Judean Hills, the crystalline sea
of the waters of eternity wherein all things exist.

8

Adah—The Daughter

As we gaze into the dark night-sky and see there the myriads of diamond stars, we may imagine their beauty as they were mirrored in the beautiful Jordan and sacred Galilee, and looked down upon Jephthah as a hero of faith, and it is not difficult to look down the cycle of time and see a brighter star appear in the East and hear an angelic choir announcing the birth of a child born to a virgin in the little town of Bethlehem just over the hill from Jerusalem, the capital of the Jewish Empire. This birth was in fulfillment of a promise of God that He would send His son to redeem the world of sin, and become a blood sacrifice for all who believed on Him.

RUTH—*The Widow*

~~~~~~

A Friend ☆ GEM: *Topaz*

THE story of Ruth is one of the most entrancingly interesting stories in the whole realm of literature, human or divine. It is an Oriental Idyll, a beautiful narrative of love and devotion, not lacking in dramatic power.

It is difficult to get the exact time of this story. The time given is 1522 B. C. and takes place during the reign of the Judges, and before the capture of Moab by the Israelites which is related as occurring in 1336, and is included in the Bible to show that *nationality* is no bar to *divine plans*. The author is supposed to be Samuel.

This lovely story is to be read in connection with the first half of Judges, and presents a picture of domestic life at that time. It is Roll No. 11 in Synagogues.

Typically, the book may be taken as a foreview of the church—Ruth as the Gentile bride of Christ; Boaz, kinsman Redeemer, type of Christ. The events recorded in the book cover a period of ten years.

It is told of Benjamin Franklin that when he was Ambassador to the Court of France, that one evening at a gather-

ing of the literati of Paris, he was asked for a reading, where-
upon he took a manuscript from out of his pocket and read
the entire book of Ruth. They began to praise it as one of the
jewels of literature, not knowing it was from the Bible.

In the prefatory passages we are given the facts concerning the people connected with the story. The land of
Bethlehem-Judah had been torn with wars, and punishment
had been meted out to the disobedient people in the way of
famine. Bethlehem was a small town nestled among the hills
of Judah, and either in this town, or the surrounding country lived Elimelech and his wife Naomi. According to an
ancient interpretation Elimelech means "God is King," while
Naomi means "God is Sweetness."

It is reasonable to suppose that Elimelech and Naomi
had been born in Bethlehem-Judah, and were married there.
Here their two sons were born. Here they live happy lives
among their people, kindred and friends, maintaining their
own sweet way of loving and serving, participating in the
Temple service, communing with the throngs and always
making friends.

Bethlehem was a noted place at this time. Bethlehem,
also now called Beit-Lahm, is a town of hallowed sacred associations. It is about five miles from Jerusalem, between
that city and Hebron. Near the town in the valley is the
very well for whose waters David is said to have longed in
Samuel 11th chapter, 23rd verse.

The Hebrew word Bethlehem means "house of bread,"
and was possibly an attempt on the part of the Hebrews to
translate the word to its earlier name of Ephrath (Gen.
35:16) which possibly means fruitful. "Bethlehem" indeed
became that which the name had promised from the first
"the house of bread" for it has always been the bread of
Angels and He, Who in His incarnation, became also the

bread of men, found His earliest earthly habitation there. Here Rachel died in giving birth to Benjamin, and was buried. Here was born Obed, the great grandfather of David. Here was also born King David, himself, and here he grew up as a shepherd lad and here he was anointed by Samuel. It was in Bethlehem that the Inn of Chimham was located (Jer. 41:17) and many scholars believe that this Inn was the very hostelry in the manger of which our Lord was born. In this town the prophet Micah (Micah 5:12) points his wonderful prediction of the birth of the Messiah. It is interesting that after the birth of Christ no other event in the New Testament appears to have taken place there and no one is recorded to have visited the city in the New Testament.

This city, while of most importance to all who have read and loved the sweet story of Ruth and Naomi, and been inspired by the story of angels announcing the birth of a newborn Babe that should become the Redeemer of mankind, and a blessing to all who believed on His name, is still hallowed.

Strange, that a famine should occur in the very place where abundant grain harvests had made the city of Bethlehem a veritable granary for the country.

Under the pressure of such calamity, a Bethlehemite by the name of Elimelech took his wife, Naomi, and their two sons, Mahlon (My God is King) and Chilion (Pining) far across the Jordan river into the land of Moab, a Gentile country and, of course, a pagan one—a dangerous thing to do.

The Moabites were interesting people. They were descendants of Lot, nephew of Abraham. They had forgotten the true God and worshipped an idol named Chamos.

A very natural thing occurred. The sons married Moabitish damsels, named Ruth and Orpah. But misfortune overtook them and in the course of about ten years all three of the men died. Whether of disease or pestilence we do not know, but there were three deaths in the home within a short time.

Naomi was far from her father's God, and far from her home and the forms of worship she loved so well. She had kept up the worship of Jehovah, and now in her loneliness, she longed for the consolation of those gracious ceremonies that immortalized the Hebrew race. She longed for her kinsman and friends, and at last her heart turned back to home, and in her spirit surged the love that came into her soul when she was a maiden in Bethlehem.

She divulged her longings to her daughters-in-law. She told them her own people were strangers to them, and in their own land and among their own people they should remain while she journeyed back to Bethlehem. She feared her farm land might have become alienated, and also that her absence had brought many obstacles which they might not be able to conquer. Therefore, she urged them to remain in the land of their nativity while she returned alone to her own country and to her own people.

According to the Jewish law, when a man died leaving his widow, his next of kin, brother, or near kin should take the widow in order to raise the children who would bear the same family name and inherit the property. In her bitterness over the loss of her two sons, Naomi told her daughters-in-law that she had nothing to give them as her sons had died, and she had no more sons to give. She exclaimed, "The hand of Jehovah has gone against me," but she felt that she must return to her own land. She bade them remain in their own country, and marry some desirable men and be happy—she could not be happy, but she wanted them to be.

Orpah thought of her family ties, of her gods, of her

companions, and possibly of another husband from her own people, and returned to her home. But Ruth, in a poetic reply of great beauty and feeling, refused to leave Naomi in her sorrow. Embracing her mother-in-law she exclaimed:

> "Entreat me not to leave thee,
>   Or to return from following after thee:
>   For whither thou goest, I will go;
>   And where thou lodgest, I will lodge:
>   Thy people shall be my people,
>   And thy God my God:
>   Where thou diest, will I die,
>   And there will I be buried:
>   The Lord do so to me, and more also,
>   If ought but death part thee and me."

The parting with Orpah must have been sad, and as she retraced her steps over the stones and mounds of the fertile valleys and fields of Moab, we wonder if her heart did not ache with the burden of parting from the gentle Naomi. We are told no more of Orpah, but the history of Ruth has come down through the ages. Her choice made that day had decided for all the world that which all men acknowledge as wisdom and strength.

We wonder if, in our thinking, we have ever come to understand the full measure of a choice that forever affects our human destiny. None of us is aware what human interests hang upon a decision, or what destiny has in store for us upon taking a road to the right or to the left.

No storms or tempest of life could sever Ruth from the one she loved. And this was love, not in the sense of love between man and wife, mother and son or daughter, but love of a FRIEND, that majestic love that glorified the ties between Jonathan and David, that love which has been written about in the tongue of every spoken language of all countries on earth where the beautiful story of Ruth has been told.

By this choice Ruth did not know that she was destined to become the mother of the ancestral line of Jesus of Nazareth. We are not told of the long journey to Bethlehem, or how the journey was made—whether on foot, or the back of the friendly camel, or helped along the way by travellers. But we are brought at once to the scene in Bethlehem where the friends of Naomi welcomed her and carried the news all about town of the arrival of their friend, now destitute, and of the misfortune that had befallen her in the land of Moab; also, the news that she had brought back with her a beautiful daughter-in-law.

Naomi's grief over the loss of her husband and sons was apparent. She, in her sorrow, exclaimed, "Call me not Naomi, call me Mara," which means *bitter,* for verily her heart yearned for her dead.

In the development of the story, we find that Ruth remained with Naomi, working for the support of herself and her aged mother-in-law. Naomi told her how to act, how to speak, and how to dress. The beautiful climax comes in the marriage of Ruth to Boaz, a wealthy farmer of that community.

This was brought about by the old custom of allowing the poor to glean in the fields at harvest time. Naomi had nothing to give Ruth, but she chose wisely and well for her by sending her into the fields of the best class people, and coaching her in manners and actions.

Boaz was a cousin of Elimelech, Naomi's husband, and was of marked ancestral lineage. He was the son of Rahab, the woman in whose house the spies of Joshua lodged. She was a Gentile, but when she heard of the story of the crossing of the Red Sea, and of God's dealing with the Children of Israel, feeding them upon manna in the wilderness, she gave her heart to God, and when the spies came into Jericho she protected them. She later married Salmon, and Boaz was a son of this marriage.

By a legal rite in which a shoe was exchanged, Boaz' marriage to Ruth was made possible, although he was not her next in kin according to law.

Ruth's marriage to Boaz resulted in the birth of a son whom they called Obed. How the heart of Naomi rejoiced when she held this child in her arms, and when she heard Ruth say, "Take him and raise him for me, for I have loved thee more than ten daughters," her heart was again full of happiness. Obed was the father of Jesse, who was the father of David. David was the father of Solomon the wisest of men. In direct lineage we find that the promised Messiah came from Ruth.

Ruth is usually regarded as the heroine of the story, but the charming climax is really centered on Naomi, and Ruth is the means through which it is reached. Naomi, with her empty heart, had in the end, found consolation.

Friends—the blessedness of just friends! Have you one that you love? A friend for whom you would sacrifice? A friend in whose company you love to linger, upon whose words you love to hang? Cherish that friend. Stand by that friend, be true to that friend for every hour of your life. In times of distress, they come to you; in times of joy, they are with you; in times of woe, their words comfort you. How much is wrapped up in a hearty handclasp of a friend! How much is enwreathed in the charm of a smile! How much is enshrined in a token of goodness and graciousness in human life!

Do you want to know how to succeed? Be friendly, be gracious, be kind, appreciate your friends and their friendships. "Be ye kindly affectioned one toward another." Sorrow always comes to those who betray their friends. Remember the friendship of Ruth in all your dealings with your friends. By the accumulation of friendships we enrich our days of old age, gathering here a little and there a little, so that when we come to the last days of "Memories" our hearts are made glad by reviewing the closeness of the love that had bound us together with our friends.

In Bunyan's *Pilgrim's Progress* the Interpreter said to Mercy, "Thy setting out is good, for thou hast given credit to the truth; thou art a Ruth, who did for the love she bare to Naomi, and the Lord her God, leave the land of her nativity, to come out, and go with a people that she knew not heretofore."

And so, we may have to leave some of our most cherished things in the way of thoughts and habits, and actions, to become a true FRIEND.

Sign and emblem

When bound together into a sheaf, the smallest actions of love and service make a strong appeal. Patient industry receives its own reward.

Both sign and flower of Ruth have been changed from the older rituals. Instead of holding sheaves of barley the hands now are extended closed, thus imitating the action of Ruth.

The flower has been changed from the sunflower to the yellow jessamine.

There are two kinds of jessamine—the sturdy bush, and the twining vine. Let us suppose that Ruth was sturdy in her desire to remain with Naomi, and twining about her mother-in-law a friendship that proved to be lasting and well worthwhile as history had proved.

COLOR

The symbolic color of Ruth is yellow.

It is the color of the rising sun, which kisses the sleepy world a gracious "Good Morning."

It is color of ripened grain, thanking heaven for the privilege of furnishing daily bread.

It is the color of the goldenrod, the buttercup, the heart of the daisy, the sunflower. The brush of artists can only imitate this beautiful color.

It is the color of the hair of a child as it ripples over a smile-wreathed face of innocence.

It is the color of the noonday sun gleaming on the harvest fields, and the golden harvest moon as it shines on the waving fields of grain.

It is the color of the paved streets of heaven and the sheen of wings of the angelic choir.

It greets us the first thing in the morning, and shines through the noonday's heat. It dips in mid-ocean as a farewell at the close of the day, and reflects back its beams of glory always inspirational and holy. By the bonds of garnered friendships, we lay up golden memories, and garner precious sheaves for our old age.

ESTHER—*The Wife*

~~~~~~

A Star   ☆   GEM: *Diamond*

THE book of Esther is found in the Old Testament, between the books of Nehemiah and Job. Time 474 B. C.

It takes up the narrative of the Jews in their scattered
and diversified life after the fall of Samaria. This crisis in
their history was brought about by Nebuchadnezzar, King of
Babylon. Their captivity in Babylon lasted for seventy years,
or until the first year of the reign of King Cyrus.

The entire book is given to the story of Jewish experiences culminating in the overthrow of the oppressor through
the instrumentality of a Jewish maiden—Esther.

Manuscripts of the Book of Esther are more numerous
than of any other portion of the Old Testament. The Book
of Esther is found in all complete private Bible codices; it is
also appended to the law in most sacred, or synagogue rolls.
So high is the esteem which this book enjoys among the Jews
that every family is anxious to own it in the form of the manuscript prescribed by the Talmud for reading at Purim. This has
led to an immense number of "Esther Rolls" that are often

masterpieces of illuminative arts, and are encased in gold and silver cases of exquisite workmanship.

The exquisite oriental story of Esther begins directly with the magnificent banquet which Ahasuerus, the king, gave in his palace of Shushan. The story is of a Jewish maiden and how she became the queen of Ahasuerus, king of Persia, and saved her people from destruction planned against them by Haman, the king's favorite. Ahasuerus is the celebrated ruler Xerxes, a sensual, self-indulgent occupant of the throne, who endeavored to subjugate Greece. This fact has been settled by decipherment of the Persian monument. The capital city of Ahasuerus is Susa, or Shushan—meaning "lily." It was probably built upon a hill, an acropolis, like other Eastern cities.

In the transition of historic events we find that Rome and Athens had been made Republics, tribunes had been created, the great battle of Maranthan had been fought and Xerxes had become King. His wealth and power had greatly increased so that he was known afar. The Persians at this time were highly civilized in the ways then known. Warfare was carried on with all surrounding nations. Spoils, including captives were carried away by the conquering army. The battles of Salamis and Thermopyle were fought and Athens burned by the Persians. Greece had been invaded and the Athenians driven from its shores. Aristides and Socrates had been born, and in these turbulent times of warfare, pillage and plunder, the Jews were driven hither and thither—captives, slaves and sometimes free in a way, until they were finally carried to Babylon and their own kingdom totally destroyed. This is recorded under the history of Samaria. Four hundred and seventy-four years before Christ, Xerxes ruled the Kingdom of Persia. By repeated conquests, acquisitions and natural resources, the kingdom had grown immensely wealthy, so much so that the palaces of the King were marvels of beauty. The King's throne was made of gold and ivory. Royalty reveled in wealth and wickedness. Women were kept in wanton splendor, subject to the caprices of the King.

In Shushan, the capital city, the King's palace was a house of wonder. The courts were hung with draperies of white and green and blue, which were fastened with cords of fine linen and purple, to silver rings, and pillars of marble. The beds were of gold and silver upon pavements of red and blue and white marble. Drinking cups were of gold, and no two alike. Royal wine was dispensed with lavish extravagance.

Among the captives carried from Palestine was a man named Mordecai, who had not returned with the first pilgrimage to the homeland. There was also a little girl, born in Persia, whom Mordecai had reared because she was orphaned and alone. He became her guardian and taught her in all the ways of his homeland. Hadassah was a beautiful child and had grown up to be a lovely maiden.

Mordecai had been made Hebrew Minister at the Court of Persia and was a favored servant of the King, so much so that his place was one of envy.

Mordecai had reared Hadassah as his own daughter, who, in some biblical way, is now called Esther. Her father had been killed in one of the numerous battles, and her uncle took her as his own.

Having lived—though a captive—amid the luxurious surroundings of the Palace, she naturally absorbed much of the stateliness and dignity necessary for a great woman, and being taught by her uncle in all the rudiments of Jewish doctrines, and heredity lore, she was fitted for the great future before her, but as entirely innocent of aspirations as the dewdrop on the purest flower.

She no doubt had seen the great Queen Vashti, with her ladies in waiting, and their costly robes but, being a captive maiden only, looked on in wonder at the display of wealth and grandeur, little dreaming that greater than this was to be hers.

In the third year of the reign of Xerxes, the Ahasuerus of the Bible—in order to display his great wealth to the Nation, called his chamberlains, princes and lords together and planned a feast that was to last for days.

Not to be outdone Queen Vashti called her ladies in waiting and her women of the court together and planned a feast to rival that of her lord and master. The splendor of the Queen's feast was not to overshadow the feast of the King, but to equally show to the women of the land the entire wealth of all the king's house.

On the seventh day of the feast, the King, when his heart was merry with wine, forgetting for the time the customs of the nation and the "law of the Medes and Persians," and especially the law of the King's Palace, caused summoned into the presence of himself and his drunken Lords and Princes, the Queen of his kingdom. Knowing full well that the law of the palace which prohibited even the Queen to come into the presence of the King unsummoned, partly because she wished her dignity to remain unchallenged, and mostly because she was Queen and must therefore be an example for her women, she refused to obey the summons, and thereby aroused the indignation of the King.

After calling a Council of Princes, it was agreed that her example would be copied by the women of the realm and all wives would soon forget to be obedient to their husbands. Queen Vashti was promptly divorced and banished from the place.

After the King had duly sobered he bethought himself of

22

the lovely Queen and grew remorseful, because he loved her. Again his advisers came to him and persuaded him that it would be better for him to bring to the courts the most beautiful maiden that could be found. A search was instituted for a maiden that would prove to be more beautiful than the lovely Vashti and possess the womanly virtues necessary for a queen.

Mordecai at once brought the beautiful Esther as a candidate, but carefully concealed the fact of her descent from the Jewish race. Beautiful of form and face, pure in mind and heart, she needed little of the physical culture that was given to the women awaiting the choice of the King. For six months she was massaged and bathed in oils and myrrh, and six months in perfumed and costly ointments to make her more physically perfect, and when attired in the superbly elegant white robes furnished by her uncle, she went in the evening into the presence of the King, and so pleased him that he at once proclaimed her Queen, and made a feast, gave gifts, released prisoners, and reveled in wealth to his heart's content.

In the course of years, the King's life, at one time, was in jeopardy through some treachery. Mordecai informed the Queen, who at once communicated to the King his danger. This cemented his love for her, and he promised her that at any time she needed his protection for herself, to remind him of this and he would grant her request even to the half of his kingdom.

The Jews were increasing in numbers as were their enemies, and in due course of time the enemies became powerful and numerous. At the court was one who was very jealous of Mordecai, who had grown much in favor with the King owing to his relation to the Queen.

Resorting to treachery, this enemy—Haman, Prime

Minister to the King—used methods so common in politics of any kind, where an office of distinction is concerned, and caused an edict to be sent forth that upon a given date all Jews should be put to death.

After issuing the proclamation, the King found written upon the chronicles of Media and Persia that Mordecai, through Esther, had saved his life. His gratitude for his own safety led him to cause greater elevation to Mordecai, which so incensed Haman that his evil mind set about with political intrigue to bring about a total extermination of the Jews, thus getting Mordecai out of his way. He sent the proclamation by messenger to all parts of the kingdom, and Jews were to be slain wherever found.

Mordecai's grief over this proclamation can well be imagined. He sent court messengers to Queen Esther carrying news of the proclamation, but she sent back word that she was powerless owing to the laws of the palace. Again the messenger returned to the sorrowing Queen, carrying word from Mordecai, reminding her that if all Jews perished, she herself would perish as she was a Jew, and being Queen would not save her.

He also reminded her that perhaps God had brought her to the kingdom for just such a time as this, and that she must obey His voice. He insisted that she go into the presence of the King and personally plead for her people.

When Esther understood the full import of the edict, that her own life as well as the lives of her uncle and all her people must be taken, she sent word to Mordecai that "I will go in unto the King, which is not according to the law, and if I perish, I perish."

But she did not plunge into this ordeal without preparation. She called on all Jewish women to fast with her for three days, and at the end of the three days she prayed with all her people to God for the deliverance of her people, and to point the way for her to perform her task.

The Bible story tells of the feast she had prepared for the King, and also of a second feast to which Haman was invited, and at this feast, with her diplomacy, together with her wisdom, she asked the King to reverse his cruel edict and spare her chosen people.

The ritual story dramatically gives the court scene, and final result of the request Esther made of the King. Her people were spared and Haman reaped what he had sown, in that he was hanged on the scaffold he had prepared for the hanging of Mordecai. The King gave Mordecai his official signet ring and authorized him to act next in power to the King, himself. The reign of Mordecai and Esther was long and supreme in kindness to kindred and friends.

Instead of the Jews being slain according to the edict sent out by Haman, they were prepared to defend themselves. A feast celebrating their victory was established and is kept to this time by all orthodox Jews. This feast is called the Feast of Purim and the reading of the Megillah is in both the home and synagogue. This narrative thus read or told is one of the most striking and most effective stories of the world. And to all, both Jew and Gentile, the Book of Esther is an intelligent story of itself, having roots deep in the history of the Jewish race.

The signet ring of the King of Persia is spoken of in *Arabian Knights*.

The lesson is designed to teach us the beauties of self-sacrifice. Esther could have kept her identity secret and preserved her own life, but she chose for her people and with her own people and risked losing her crown rather than to see them destroyed, and she lost nothing in being true to her race.

In reading the Book of Esther, it will be seen that chapter 9, verses 26–28 tell of the institution of the feast of Purim (Lots) which arose out of the rejoicing of the Jews in being so signally delivered from their enemies on the 13th day of Adar, in the 12th year of King Ahasuerus (Xerxes) B.C. 473.

It was this day that Haman had chosen by Lot (Pur, Esther 3–7) on which to exterminate the Jews throughout the Persian Empire. It was enjoined by Mordecai that this feast should be kept yearly on the 14th and 15th of Adar. It is kept to this day by all Jews.

This story is told in all synagogues, homes around firesides, and in all countries wherever Jews have wandered and are together by ties deep-rooted in their hearts and repeated at each Feast of Purim or Feasts of Lots.

The book of Esther contains but ten chapters and may be read at one sitting. To obtain all the leading facts of this lesson one must read not only the entire ten chapters, but fit the events told therein with ancient history. But our lesson to be learned is plain. We sometimes see people elected or elevated to positions of honor who soon become so puffed up over their elevation that they forget their friends, forget the circumstances previous to the elevation, and thus become arrogant and unthankful and often domineering, utterly without discretion, and without the natural qualities necessary for positions of high esteem. Such persons are unfitted for position of honor, and reflect upon whatever position they may hold much discredit both to themselves and to their friends.

Esther was not so. Her head was not turned. She wore the crown with becomingness of a Queen, and when called upon was equal to the occasion, even though it meant, perhaps, the stripping away all that had placed her in the exalted position. It was a most beautiful surrender, and one well worth emulation. We should so live that when we, too, are called upon to make sacrifices for our friends, we may, in a measure, partake of the virtues of this noble Queen, forgetting self and selfish ambitions to help our friends. If we desire a crown, we must earn it.

This lesson is also designed to teach us that we must fulfill our own destiny—or be total failures.

There is a well defined duty for each of us, and when personal pride, personal ambition or personal aggrandizement are conquered, we rise to the best there is in us, and act from inward impulse more as God wills than at any other time. It sometimes takes sorrow—deep and crushing—to wring from us the jewels of God's implanting, but they are buried deep within the heart of each of us, and await their discovery by those who are obedient to the demands of justice which must be tempered with mercy.

Esther's story is an example to youth, to married women and to all who prize purity of mind and purpose, and to all who keep themselves unspotted from the world. A man wants his wife to be spotless, he wants his daughter to be above reproach, he wants his sister pure and chaste, he wants his mother to live in his memory as one who is pure and spotless. The world needs Esthers today—as well as at this time in the history of Persia.

To live a life so broad, so deep and so pure that the malicious tongue cannot mar, and with a mind and heart pure and kept free from contamination of pride and conceit, should be the goal of every woman.

THE SIGN AND EMBLEM

An appeal to intelligence, heart emotion, and world activity, guided by Jehovah.

The sign is an appeal to the intellect, the understanding, and to the heart or honest principles of humanity. The two motions are an appeal and direction.

The emblems are explained in the lecture.

COLOR

The symbolic color is white, one of the emblematic colors of Masonry which is preserved in the apron and gloves with which the initiate is invested.

It is the symbol of innocence and purity. The white vesture as may be seen throughout this work was a part of the ancient mysteries.

The flower chosen for this point is the lily, pure and spotless, giving of its beauty and loveliness to the hills of Palestine, so much so that Jesus said, "Behold the lilies of the field. They toil not neither do they spin, and yet I say unto you that even Solomon in all his glory was not arrayed like unto one of these."

"These are they which have come up through great trials and tribulations, having their robes washed white in the blood of the Lamb."

Keep your robe white—unspotted from the world's contamination.

MARTHA—*The Sister*

〰〰〰〰〰〰〰〰〰〰〰〰〰〰〰〰〰〰〰

Instructed by Christ   ☆   Gem: *Emerald*

These things we gather from the story of Martha:
She was friendly, her home was open to others.
Martha was a hard-working, effective homekeeper.
Martha loved and trusted Jesus and wanted to show it.
There was no selfishness in Martha's nature.
Her faith was firm in the hour of trial.

Only two detailed accounts of Martha are found in the Bible, Luke 11:17–46; John 11. Luke 10 gives an incident in her home life.

Martha's religion was as it should be—the center of her life.

Religion should be as true as science, as beautiful as art, and as vital as life.

Martha is the first of the heroines taken from the New Testament, and the story sets forth an example of trustful faith, belief in the divinity of Jesus, hope of a future existence, love and sympathy for humanity, and fellowship of friends, and promulgates the doctrine of the Trinity.

One and one-half miles from Jerusalem, just over the

Mount of Olives, there nestled a little town whose inhabitants were restful as the peaceful valley. Bethany is near Mount Olivet, north of Jericho. Under a tall tower there is a vault, said to be the tomb of Lazarus.

In the town there lived a family of three—two sisters and a brother, who were known to all who chanced to pass through on their way up to Jerusalem to attend the feasts. The family was known for its genial hospitality and restful atmosphere. The members of the family were of the average kind and gave cheer to all who passed their way.

In His journeyings, Jesus found this small home, and its atmosphere proving to be the needed tonic for His turbulent spirit, He many times sought this house as an abode—or refuge after days of labor.

Here, a feast was once prepared for Him and His followers. Here, at one time the crowd became so great that Martha insisted that her sister Mary assist her with the serving. Here, Jesus won many followers and among them Lazarus, Mary and Martha were the first. Here, Jesus did much of His teaching, and Mary was an intent listener to His doctrines. He must have explained to them all the prophecies relating to His coming, and to have guided them into a belief that was soon to be their testing.

This belief was not shaken even though Lazarus was taken sick during the absence of Jesus, died and was buried, and seemingly all hope gone for his earth life. Paid mourners stood about the door or sat near the tomb. The sisters were bowed with grief and torn with longings for their brother whom they had seen placed behind the sealed door of the tomb.

But Martha's faith was not shaken even though the Master had not come when called upon before the death of

30

Lazarus. Her faith held through the mockings of the paid mourners, and the doubts of Mary. When word was brought that the Master was coming across the mountains, she prepared to go to meet Him. As He came down the olive-bordered road, with its tall cedars whispering in the breezes, His heart was torn with grief for the family so bereft, but He knew God's plan was best, and a doubting public must have the sign they had clamored for.

Martha hastened out to meet Him. Her salutation was not the salaam of the Sadducee, or the frigid bow of the Pharisee, but the worshipful attitude of a devotee of the God Divine.

With her hands raised in supplication, she cried—and oh the piteous wail of that cry and the heartbeats of the world in that wail; how many of the human family of today have felt this appeal—"Lord, if thou hadst been here, my brother had not died, but I know that even now, whatsoever thou wilt ask of God he will give it to thee."

No one knows the keenness of soul sorrow save those who have given their loved ones to the tomb. The answer came in solemn tones:

"Thy brother shall rise again."

"Yea," answered Martha, "I know that he will rise at the resurrection of the last day."

"I," answered Jesus, "am the resurrection and the life. He that believeth on me though he were dead, shall live again, and he that liveth and believeth on me shall never die."

Thus comforted, Martha followed the Master to the tomb. Here they found a numerous crowd, mourners, friends and associates. Seeing their sympathy and His own heart full of human sympathy, He commanded the stone be rolled away, and in spite of protests that Lazarus had been dead

31

four days, the stone was rolled backward and Lazarus walked forth wrapped in his grave clothes.

The people had asked for a sign. They received it in the raising of Lazarus—the sign of the resurrection and reunion of soul and body, the mortal and the immortal.

Many sects and creeds were in existence. Teachers of the Pharisees, Sadducees, Herodians, etc., had been created by the diversified rulers, and the conglomerate peoples living in and about Jerusalem and other cities of Palestine had become so upset that to hold fast to any doctrine made one a target for all the rest.

The "Soul Sleepers," the "Self-righteous," the "Idolatrous," and "Chaldeac," and "Romanistic" doctrines had permeated all the provinces, so that when the new religion (or Christ Religion) had been advocated by Jesus, Himself, and His followers, the people were loathe to leave off their old doctrines and accept the new.

Jesus taught the doctrine of life after death, and His followers adhered to this belief. He had told them of His own Divinity, and connection with the Father, and His followers were made to realize this by His many acts of Divine power.

His willingness to go with the sisters to the tomb of Lazarus and thereby show, not only His Divine sympathy for humanity, but His power over death which established once and for all His mediatorship between God and man, was evident.

The belief in a future existence is co-existent with the human race. It antedates the apostles and the prophets; it is older than Moses and Abraham and goes back beyond the days of Noah.

But to see the evidence of the soul reunited with the body even after four days of separation, was a sign that even the most skeptical had not dared to dream.

32

Sign and Emblem

When properly given this sign is a perfect Triangle. A Triangle represents the God-head.

The very first verse of the Bible gives the ultimatum of the Doctrine of the Trinity. The Hebrew word translated "God" is plural. The three persons in the God-head are:

God, the Father
God, the Son
God, the Holy Spirit.

God, the Father, the first person in the God-head, is the one who rules; God, the Son, the second person in the God-head, is the one through whom everything is created; God, the Spirit, the third person in the God-head, is the one who develops to completion that which is created by things material.

The broken column is a fitting emblem of a life cut off in the fullness of vigor. A life shorn of the dreams of youth, and of the imperfections of physical man, compared with the perfection of God.

There are more tragedies bound up in the human heart that can be found in leather-bound, gilt-edged books— tragedies of broken hearts, of wrecked homes, of blighted lives, and ruined prospects, of blasted fortunes, and benighted lives. Buried deep in the human heart, covered by bodies that must be kept going, there is a great big ache caused by some wrong. The unshed tear, the leaden sighs, the hopeless countenances are often caused by disappointment or some buried hope.

"O, the world is dying for a little bit of love."

33

The sympathetic tear of Jesus at the tomb of Lazarus should be a dynamo that would compel the human family to sympathize, and live to love, and love to live.

> "He wept that we might weep,
> Each wrong demands a tear."

The hope for the future existence of the soul is the inspiration of all good deeds, and the installation of the fear of evil. The hope of meeting with loved ones in the heavenly shores inspires the mind to noble deeds of love and sacrifice. The fear of punishment for evil deeds keeps many in the path of rectitude and right. The approval of conscience or the lashings of remorse are nature's guides along life's pathway.

A belief in the Divinity—of a life after death—is the strongest magnet to right. A belief in a Divinity that has the power to give and the power to take away, to bless or to curse, to love, to protect, to guide, and to save our souls from death, is the lesson to be learned from Martha.

"To die is but to live"—and with what glorious rapture, when we meet and greet our loved ones who have gone before.

Masonry bases its Drama of Faith upon the merits of the Lion of the Tribe of Judah, which strengthens it with confidence and composure to look forward to a blessed immortality.

Two thousand years have passed since Jesus stood at the grave in Bethany. Yet, today, over the chasm of centuries there comes to us that eternal challenge:

"I am the resurrection and the life. He that believeth in me though he were dead, yet shall he live again; and whosoever liveth and believeth in me shall never die. Believest thou this?"

34

Martha—The Sister

The sign of Martha is a recognition of the Divinity of Christ—as the One High Priest, the Mediator.

COLOR

Green is the ever-quickening cloak of nature, the symbol of eternity.

God clothed the earth in green so that our eyes will be rested when we behold a landscape, or gain strength from the trees and hills. "I will look up to the hills from whence cometh my strength, my strength cometh from the Lord who made heaven and the earth." The green leaf, the spray of the fern, the twig of evergreen, all remind us that through nature's unrobing lives God's plan that all shall be clothed with Christ's righteousness if we walk in His ways, and are clothed with His love.

ELECTA—*The Mother*

~~~~~~

Called of God   ☆   Gem: *Ruby*

It has been said that the lesson of Electa is a Catholic legend.

Search has been made for the authenticity of this, but so far nothing has been found.

We come, therefore, back to the lesson as it is given, in older rituals, and for what it may teach.

The word "Electa" translated means "overseer," or "called of God," or "superintendent."

We gather, then, that in the early Christian era Electa was called of God to superintend a flock of early Christians in her part of the country. This flock may have been in her own home.

By her noble example and faithful service and leadership she became known far and near and thus was a target for much persecution.

John, the beloved disciple of our Master, addressed his Second Epistle to the Elect Lady and her children.

In the Greek version we find the word "Kyria," which may be translated as a proper name. It was a very common name among the Greeks, and it refers here to some notable Saint in the neighborhood of Ephesus who ministered to John in his old age.

The letter is brief, for the writer is soon to make a visit to this Sister in Christ, and to speak with her face to face. In the letter he commends her for her perseverance and asks that she continue in that commandment "love one another." The burden of the letter is love—not a passion, or an emotion, but as a life, whose abiding influence will permeate throughout the world.

A beautiful story of Electa and her heroism has been written by an O. E. S. writer, but this author has drawn upon her imagination so much that the golden thread that has been woven into the Bible story is lost sight of, and our sympathies go out to Electa, the woman, and not Electa, the called of God.

In adopting the Christian religion, Electa had adopted all the virtues and graces that flow out of it. She spent her large income in relieving the destitute, and in every way proved that she lived to serve.

The ritual story tells in brief of her persecution, and her bravery in holding steadfast to her faith, and the doctrines as taught her by the beloved John.

Several years had elapsed since the crucifixion, death and resurrection of the Master.

Many divisions had arisen concerning the final destiny of the soul, and the Divinity of Christ, and to answer all these absorbing questions, St. John wrote his Epistles.

St. John was one of the Twelve Apostles and had accompanied Jesus on many important occasions. He was with Him at the raising of the mother of Peter's wife. He was with Him at the transfiguration, and among those who saw the final ascension. He was one of the three to whom had been vouchsafed the most minute teachings of Jesus. He understood thoroughly and gives graphically and most interestingly his message.

His Gospel message begins, "In the beginning was the Word, and the Word was with God, and the Word was God, the same was in the beginning with God. All things were made by Him, and without Him was not anything made. In Him was life; and the life was the light of men. The light shineth in darkness and the darkness comprehended it not."

This was, figuratively speaking, of the teachings of Jesus and the perversity of the reception of His teachings.

John's Gospel, his general Epistle and his Epistle to the Elect Lady and his Epistle to Gaius are all full of the word "LOVE," its manifold uses and purposes.

His apocalypse is a message full of symbolic word pictures and a strong treatise on love in its application by the Christ, and of promises to the faithful.

He understood his subject thoroughly. His writings all have a double predicate and a triplicate imperative—Love God; Love your Neighbor; Love not the world.

It is a well-known fact that the last days of John, the beloved Disciple, were spent at Ephesus. Nero, Emperor of Rome, was an eccentric, a madman, and in his great egotistic manner wanted no one to be more powerful or influential than he. Therefore, he resorted to every means of eradicating the followers of Christ, even persecuting them in such brutal manner that his own people began to take notice of it. At last, he caused Rome to be set on fire and took this advantage of laying it at the door of the Christians, so that the people would become more incensed against them.

Nero threw some of them into dungeons, others he fed to hungry lions, still others he covered with pitch and nailed them on lamp posts as burning street lights. Floggings, scourgings, flaying alive, crucifying, and other means of torture were resorted to in order to entirely eradicate the Christians. But in spite of all this, in dens and caves some of them lived and helped and held to their teachings and some others flew to other countries less antagonistic and there carried on their teachings.

The ritual lesson gives briefly the trials of one of the Christians. And we find Electa ripening daily for the better world. Her fame had gone everywhere, as Electa, the mother of the faithful, the friend of the distressed.

And now her trial came. Strict orders were issued by the Roman Emperor that all who professed the name of Christ should recant or suffer death. It was not possible for so shining a mark as Electa to escape. Therefore a band of soldiers passed through the doors so long opened for the entrance of the poor and distressed. But the captain of the band was loathe to injure one whose deeds he had heard so much about. He told her that recantation was a mere form, and need not affect her private life or opinion, and handed her a cross which he bade her throw on the floor and put her foot upon it, assuring her if she did this he would then leave her without danger.

Electa took the cross, but it was to press it with ardor to her bosom, to her lips, to weep tears of love upon it, to assure the soldiers that in this sign she was more willing to die, and from the hour she professed the Christ religion, she had waited for this opportunity to testify her love for her Christ. She told them to do their duty whatever it was, and Christ would give her divine grace to do hers.

Our sympathies would fain close here, before the drama reached the final act; tragical and horrible as it was, but painful as the task, we will, for the sake of completing the history, paint the sad end in as moderate colors as the vivid subject will allow.

The family was cast into prison, a loathsome dungeon, where they remained for a year, at the end of which time the Roman Judge came in person and besought them yet, as it was not too late, to save their lives by recanting from the faith. But Electa made answer as before, as did all the family, saying, "It is good that we, for whom Christ died, give testimony to the power of His death by dying for Him."

Then came the last sad scene. They were taken from the dungeon and severely scourged—mother, father and children—until life barely lingered in their tortured bodies. Then they were taken in carts drawn by oxen, amid the jeers and scorn of the people, to the nearest hill, and one by one nailed to crosses. The heroism never left them, and they all died martyrs to their faith, as meek and loving servants of Christ. The last words of Electa was a prayer for the pardon of her persecutors.

We cannot carry on the teachings of this lesson unless we practice the principles of the virtues as taught by Electa— that we love one another.

Moreover, if persecutions come our way, we should be noble in combating their influences, and practice the law laid down in the Golden Rule.

We do not know how long we may be able to enjoy the present freedom of worshipping God according to the dictates of our own conscience, and we should fully appreciate the lesson of Electa. If persecutions of this nature happen to us, by the grace of God, we may be able to stand firm in the faith once delivered to the Saints.

If persecutions of a personal nature come, then we should be strong in the virtue of patience and forbearance remembering that

"Truth, crushed to earth will rise again,
The eternal years of God are hers;
But error, wounded, writhes in pain
And dies amid her worshippers."

The Thirteenth Chapter of Second Corinthians should be read in connection with this lesson. Love is the base of all good, whether counted by days or by years. God is above all and in all. The motive behind all our actions should be the dynamo of love.

The lesson of Electa is taken from persons living in the same era in which we live. Her desire to be steadfast in her religion and the teachings of John, the Divine, should inspire us to be steadfast in these days of trial.

The lesson is also a combination of all that has gone before. Here, we have the unveiled eyes to see the right; the outstretched hands to help; the intelligence and understanding mind to do; the divine faith to believe and the willingness to suffer, if necessary, persecutions, and thus we are brought to the final great commandment that "We love one another."

If these lessons are properly inculcated into our lives, and the warmth of their power made to blossom forth in our everyday acts, the fruit will be love and friends, firm and true. And, as a final reward, we may hope to be among the faithful to whom it will be said, "I was sick and ye gave me a couch; I was lame and ye gave me a crutch; I was blind and ye physicianed my eyesight; I was orphaned and ye brought me home—inasmuch as ye did it to one of the least of these, ye did it unto me also."

Sign and Emblem

Electa refused to cast the cross upon the ground. Instead she firmly clasped it to her breast.

Just where the cross came into existence, or how, there is a deep mystery. When man emerged from the darkness of antiquity he emerged with a cross upon his breast. No one knows how it got there, or why, but the cross in one form or another has long been a symbol of something divine. No sect or creed has a monopoly on the cross. It belongs to all humanity.

The cross, though it has at its heart a collusion and a contradiction, can extend its four arms forever without altering its shape. Because it has a paradox at its center it can grow without changing. The cross opens its arms to the four winds. It is significant to travelers.

It was reared in the wilderness for the Hebrew race to "Look and Live"; it was reared on Calvary for the same reason; it was carried by the early Crusaders, and left its mark in the panels of doors; it has become the emblem of the Christian religion.

There are three forms of the cross—the cross of St. Andrew, used on the flag of Scotland; the cross of St. George, used on the flag of England; and the Christian Cross.

It would appear that the cross of St. Andrew comes nearer to the Christian Cross represented by the arms in this lesson. The crossed arms, with the heart for a center, makes a complete pentagon, if we include the head. It would thus seem that in Electa all previous lessons are combined as the heart of all.

By extending the arms upward and outward, placing the feet in same positions downward, we have the same cross. Using the head as one point, we again see the pentagon by drawing lines from hand to head, from head to hand, from hand to foot, etc. We thus see a combination of all faculties of the spiritual as well as the natural body. These lines represent the five senses, the outer doors through which man receives his education—seeing, hearing, touching, tasting and smelling; within the mind of man there is their spiritual meaning.

The heart represented by the Altar, seat of emotion, receives its liberation from the five senses.

The cup is an Old Testament image used in the New Testament to signify man's lot, as holding what God pours out for him.

The cup, emblem of the human body, contains the blood and within this the vital fluid of life.

In the Old Testament the cup is used to express joy, comfort, happiness as well as desolation, wrath of God. In the New Testament it is noticeable that this figure is used only in reference to suffering.

Christ used this in the Garden of Gethsemane. He had previously used it in checking the ambitions of John and James.

All through the ages its symbolic meaning has been a receptacle—a chalice. It may hold evil as well as good. It may contain condemnation as well as pardon, grief or gladness.

It may be an urn of memory, a receptacle for garnered treasures, or of life's experiences.

In the lesson of Electa it denotes plenty—a full receptacle waiting for the opportunity to help the needy.

Color

Red, the color of the fifth point of the Star, is represented by blood, fire and wine. Blood contains the life principle. Fire is the element of purification. Wine represents the quickening essence—spirit.

SYMBOLISM

~~~~~~

SINCE time immemorial when people wanted to give evidence of some spiritual truth which they could not best express in words, they have used a symbol. There are two kinds of symbols.

1st—the natural—as trees, lions, and mountains for strength.

2nd—The institutional symbol which represents a concept which man has built up.

The flag is such a symbol and through the ages flags have been used to convey some universal truth.

A symbol always conveys an idea.

Nothing is more strange than the life of natural symbols.

Each time we view them we discern new meanings, new illusions.

The Old Testament was written in symbolic language, and recent discoveries of old writings have served to clear their meaning.

The Hebrews always wrote picturesquely. All oriental writings were written pictorially. As we gather from the symbols used in our ritualistic work, we see that a study of the hidden meanings are emphasized.

44

Symbolism

Inside the pentagon are certain symbols that should be studied for their meaning to us. They compose the center of our star which is surrounded by the symbolic pentagon, thus conveying a meaning deep and precious to all searchers after knowledge.

It will be seen that these symbols carry out the hidden meaning of the lecture to which they have been assigned, and each one of them bears a message of love and beauty.

With the altar as center of the pentagon, and the radiating star points, we see that Divine arrangement that is so conducive to a deeper study of the hidden meaning.

THE OPEN BIBLE

Symbol of direction

"The Light," the "WORD," "The Way," are all used in speaking of the Bible, and to all followers of the Way, it becomes a Light, and is the Word of all that is good and holy.

This book contains the mind of God, the state of man, the way of salvation, and the happiness of believers. Its doctrines are holy, its precepts are binding, its histories are true and the decisions are immutable.

Read it to be wise, believe it to be safe, and practice it to be holy. It is the traveler's map, the pilgrims staff, the pilot's compass, the soldier's sword and the Christian's character. Here is paradise restored, heaven opened, and the gates of hell disclosed. Christ is the grand object; our good, its design; and the glory of God, its end. It should fill the memory, rule the heart, and guide the feet. It is a mine of wealth, a paradise of glory, and a river of pleasure. It is given you in life, will be opened in the judgment, and will be remembered forever. It involves the highest responsibilities, will reward the greatest labor, and will condemn all who trifle with its sacred contents.

It is the guide of life to wayfarers on this earth who seek to know the ways of God, and his dealings with man. It is the WAY of all who remember the promises once given to man.

Symbolic names applied to Jesus:

"The Word," "The Way," "The Light"
"The Lily of the Valley"
"The Sun of Righteousness"
"The Lamb Slain for the Sins of the World"
"The Lion of the Tribe of Judah"
"The Rose of Sharon"
"The Bright and Morning Star"

Jesus was called the LION OF THE TRIBE OF JUDAH. His descent from the house of David gives a literal fulfillment of this, and His sacrificial death on the cross carries out the blood sacrifice as first given for the remission of sin.

Our belief in the Trinity, in the priesthood of our Saviour, in the beginning, growth and development of all things, in the necessity for the spilling of blood for the remission of sins, as the law given by God, Himself, to Abraham, strengthened again under Moses, fulfilled by Christ on the cross when the Lamb without spot or blemish was slain for the sins of the world, so fully explained in John 3–16, is so wonderously brought out in these lessons that anyone may see the depths of it if they so desire and will give thought to their study. As a beautiful climax to it all we find that Jesus is the "Bright and Morning Star," the One for Whom the Angelic Choir opened up their song of praise over the Judean hills, shepherds worshipped, and Wise Men came from the world's end, bringing

46

with them their gifts of gold, frankincense and myrrh—Gold for the King, Frankincense for the High Priest, and Myrrh for the Great Physician.

From the sacred pages of the Bible our lessons are taken —three from the Old Testament, and two from the New Testament.

Through the five heroines of our Order, the light from this book so penetrates the mind, that the journeyings through the labyrinth with all its mysteries should be plain. The lectures, when properly given, become vivid pictures of the heroine portrayed. The women of today, are called upon more and more to stand in the forefront of life's battles, and share with our Masonic Brothers the vicissitudes of present-day life. We need spiritual strength in order to withstand the many temptations and trials of the times.

Thus, we have all stages of life—Adah, the winter of Life; Ruth the fruitful, or harvest part of life; Esther, the summer of life; Martha, the soul or immortal part of life; and Electa, the creative part of life—these with their lessons portray the labyrinth of human life with its promises, its disappointments, its expectations, its pain and its glory—all so dependent upon the source of light—the God of all.

THE LILY OF THE VALLEY

A Symbol of the Christlike Spirit.

The Lily of the Valley, or conval lily is associated with religion and chivalry. With its beautiful blossoms, the rich green of its leaves, and its delicate fragrance, it is a fit harbinger of spring.

It grows in mute quietness of the shaded places, sending its perfume out to the breezes, and unmolested, it gives a background to all decorations where cut flowers are most needed to blend in with other flowers, of more brilliant hue.

It is typical of the meek widow who was willing to become cut from her natural associations, kindred and friends, to become a woman of adopted country and kinfolks, thus becoming the ancestress of Him, Who was called THE LILY OF THE VALLEY.

THE SUN

A Symbol of Light

The sun is the all conquering force of nature, the ruler of day, and the promoter of life and growth.

Esther became a light and power to her race, and shed abroad her influence of growth, strength and power. Her wisdom became next to that of Solomon, and as he was called the wisest of men, so was she called the wisest of women. She was the giver of strength to a crushed nation.

Jesus was called the "SUN OF RIGHTEOUSNESS," and, as an emblem of growth and power, we accept this as a symbol of strength and development, wisdom and power.

THE LAMB

A Symbol of Innocence and Humility

As meekness should be a characteristic of all who profess to know the truth and light, we readily see that this symbol means much to us. The gentleness of a little lamb, the appeal to us for assistance in helping mankind who seems to be struggling to find a way out, the tactfulness, and kindness needed to make the appeal to those who need our assistance, even as the meek and lowly Jesus assisted those about him,

48

should mean to us that Jesus was the LAMB SLAIN FOR THE SINS OF THE WORLD, innocent though he was.

THE LION

A Symbol of Strength and Power

The lion is a symbol of unyielding virtues, untrampled and untrammeled religious life, willing to suffer, if necessary, but strong in defense of our belief in what is right; tame in peace, but strong in protection.

From this we may learn to live peaceably with all mankind insomuch as is in our power, and strong in the Lord and the power of His might, but remembering that not always is the race to the swift and the battle to the strong, but that "I can do all things through Christ which strengtheneth me."

Jesus was called the LION OF THE TRIBE OF JUDAH, and to Him is given the power to Open the Book of Seven Seals.

PENTAGON

It is a well-known fact that certain lines or circles have a distinct meaning of their own. To find the hidden meaning of these lines should be the desire of every member of the Eastern Star.

From writers of the mysteries of the Orient we find that the pentagon represents the human body—the four points representing the limbs, and the single point, the head.

The five lines outside the Star represent the five outer doors by which man receives his education. These are the five senses—hearing, seeing, feeling, smelling, and tasting, and within the mind exists their duplicates.

49

The five points of the Star are employed as a symbol of five important rules to be observed:

First—That we should not withdraw our hand from one needing our help.

Second—That our feet should never halt in our pursuit of duty.

Third—That our prayers should ascend for the distressed.

Fourth—That a faithful breast conceals the faults and secrets of our friends—even as the tomb.

Fifth—That approaching evil is frequently averted by a friendly admonition.

A pentagon was the official emblem of the ring of King Solomon. The signet ring was a famous and much coveted token among the ancient Egyptians. The Sacred Beetle, and the Sphinx were their favorite devices. The Roman Emperor Augustus adopted the Egyptian device for his signet ring. Clement of Alexandria, in the second century, forbade the use of rings by Christians, saving alone, the signet ring which has ever been regarded as an emblem of faithfulness, and its possession, a mark of unquestioned confidence and esteem.

Signet rings are today the emblems of fraternal orders, and are not legitimately worn by any member of the Order until he is entitled to its enlightenment. Royal Arch members use the Triple Tau or Cornerstone; Blue Lodge, the Square and Compasses; Shriners, the Crescent; while the members of the Eastern Star have the Five-pointed Star, which includes the pentagon.

The pentagon may also be considered as outlining the five stages of man—Birth, Life, Death, Resurrection and Ascension.

Taking the figure of the pentagon, with the altar in the

center, it is a symbol of man, with his arms outstretched, feet outstretched, and heart enlightened by the word of God, represented by the Bible on the altar.

THE EQUILATERAL TRIANGLE

From time immemorial the equilateral triangle has been a symbol of Deity. It is symmetrical and perfect, and so, admirably symbolizes the Perfect Being.

In ancient times, resting on its point, this triangle was considered an emblem of a good, kind, merciful God, and was called the "Water Triangle." The equilateral triangle resting on its base represented a just and angry God, and was called the "Fire Triangle."

The equilateral triangle represents the three essential attributes of Deity—omniscience, omnipotence, and omnipresence. When these two triangles are superimposed they form a double triangle, or six-pointed star, which is often referred to as Solomon's Seal. This six-pointed star is a very ancient symbol. It is sometimes called the Shield of David. Its six points were considered to represent the spirit of understanding, wisdom, counsel, might, knowledge, and God. It is, therefore a striking emblem of Deity.

The equilateral triangle upon which so much of our work is based, represents to us the Trinity—of

> God's Almighty Power,
> God's All Knowing Wisdom,
> God's All Embracing Love.

TRIANGLE

The triangle has the basic quality of nature. Without three primary elements there is no life. Our being is composed of body, mind, and spirit. We have three distinct divisions of life—birth, life and death. Triangles are arranged to compose our central star of five points.

Seeking the reflection of the triangle symbol in the human mind, we may see it represents the human body as it is the tripod of life—body, soul, spirit, and in the complete family—father, mother, child.

Deep-seated in the human brain there is said to be a triangular body of no known physical function. The ancients càlled it the seat of the soul. Science now names it as the seat of intelligence, because it has connection with all five senses by a wonderful system of nerves, and is thus in communication with the outer world.

TRIANGULAR CHAIN

The human heart is shaped like a triangle.

When the Jews were led in captivity from Jerusalem to Babylon by Nebuchadnezzar, they were bound with triangular chains as an insult, because, to them, the triangle was a symbol of the Deity to be made use of only on sacred occasions.

Our work is mainly composed of triangles and circles, with some squares. The triangle is most used, as it is noticeable in the signs, the floor carpet and the signet.

CIRCLE

A circle stands for virtue. It is derived from the sun.

It stands for eternity, since it has no beginning or end; for perfection, since it cannot be improved upon; for eternity, and love, since it has perfection. It has its bounds.

The circle used in the winding of the labyrinth, and the

Symbolism

final march around the star, embraces first the single virtue, then all these virtues bound together, a symbol of the five cardinal virtues that should go to make up a well-rounded life.

THE LABYRINTH

Labyrinth means an edifice full of intricate windings or passages, which render it difficult to find the way from the interior to the outer entrance without a guide familiar with the place.

It is a maze, or bewildering path, through which we wander in our human life.

The first labyrinth is legendary and was said to have been built by Daedalus for King Minos of Crete, for the home of Minotaur of Greek mythology.

In our work, a candidate is never left to find her way alone, but a friend is always beside her.

THE ALTAR

There is an unwritten law that no one should cross between the Altar and the East during Chapter, except as designated in the initiatory work.

The Altar bears the Sacred Light—the Open Bible. The presiding officer represents the *Ruler of the day*; therefore, the rays from this light should not be dimmed by passage of obstacles between the force and the source.

An Altar in one form or another has been, in all ages and among all people, the center around which men have congregated in worship, to endeavor to climb upwards to higher standings and loftier ideals.

Fire was the basic element of all altars of the Ancients,

but as humanity advanced, fire evolved into LIGHT, and, later, in most all instances, where an Altar is used, the Bible has taken the place of fire and light, and very appropriately, since the Bible is the LIGHT that points to man the "WAY."

The signet

The word comes from the latin word *signum* or *sennet* meaning a sign. The O. E. S. Signet is a chart showing the emblematic star, emblematic flowers, emblems and symbols of the Order. It contains a cryptic motto.

Cabalistic

Means "secret," or "unwritten," or oral work.

The square

The Square is an ancient Masonic symbol teaching us to square our actions by the square of virtue.

The only standard for measuring the perfection of human life is that of virtue. In it are implied all those other traits that characterize the highest type of manhood.

"The face is a show window advertising and exhibiting the soul's stock of goods." Inward thoughts, as well as outward actions, stamp themselves indelibly upon the countenance, and go far toward determining character and personality.

In our work, the Square outlines the Temple of King Solomon, which was considered a perfect piece of architecture, taken from the directions for a Tabernacle whose dimensions, furnishings, altars, and hangings were given to Moses by the voice of God. The Square is emphasized in our floor work.

THE GAVEL

In ancient times the gavel referred to the hammer of the god Thor. In the hands of one chosen to rule the Chapter it is an emblem of power. Let us remember that "he who would rule must first learn the great lesson of obedience and the observance of every obligation heretofore taken; squaring his (or her) actions by the square of virtue and keeping his (or her) passions within due bounds."

Let it be a constant thought of every leader that "he only can teach who has passed through the severe school of self-discipline."

Self-control is the essential qualification of the presiding officer of the Order, and yet how difficult to attain that self-mastery which should be the goal of every life.

A SEAL

A seal is a token of proprietorship put by the owner upon his property, or it is the authentication of some statement or engagement, the official stamp that gives a document validity.

THE STAR

Seven hundred and fifty years of conquest had brought a large part of the then known world under the sovereignty of Rome. Her laws insured protection; her citizenship granted privilege; her civilization disseminated culture; and her military roads afforded arteries of communication and travel. The temple of Janus had been closed in token of the cessation of war, and the advent of peace. A knowledge of Hebrew Scripture was spreading over the earth and there was universal expectation of a delivering king. The Wise Men of the East were devoting their lives to a study of religion and science. They were the scholars of their age, the counselors of kings in statecraft. Herodotus speaks of them as a priestly class, men of rank and learning. Absorbed in the study of astrology, a belief in the stars became a part of their religion.

They believed that the destiny of individuals and of nations was written in the heavens to be read by knowledge and explained by wisdom. And so, when a star, strange to them, appeared in the East, they at once exclaimed, "This is the herald of the coming King."

The star led them to Bethlehem. "And when they were come into the house, they saw the young child with Mary his mother, and fell down and worshipped him; and when they had opened their treasures, they presented unto him gifts, gold, and frankincense, and myrrh," saying, "We have seen His star in the East and have come to worship Him."

NUMBERS

~~~~~~

In all the Eastern Star work we find that numbers are used to convey certain ideas, or plans.

The round number "seven" as used by the Ancients is only hinted, but wherever the number comes, we will notice that the idea plays no small part.

Thus, we have the numbers "three," "five," and "seven" many times in our work. These may or may not be significant of the many virtues of the lesson learned, but it is wise to make a proper study of them.

In the opening service, when the Matron asks the duties of the officers, each responds with three duties she has to perform, with the exception of the Secretary and Patron who each has five duties.

There are eleven small circles in the Labyrinth, one large circle and one square.

There are two guides and seven instructors.

The Order of the Eastern Star is dedicated to three things: Charity, Truth and Loving Kindness. From these emanate the five virtues exemplified by the Heroines of the Order—Obedience to the demands of Honor, Humility, Purity, Faith, and Love.

The government is vested in three bodies—the General Grand Chapter; the Grand Chapter; and the Subordinate Chapter.

The degrees of Ruth, Martha and Electa have each one emblem, while those of Adah and Esther have two each.

SIGNIFICANCE OF NUMBERS

In our studies please note the significance of numbers.

ONE—Unit; source; parent of all—GOD; one God; one faith; one baptism.

TWO—Incompleteness, but necessary to first complete number. Dependence upon ONE but productive—Man and wife, product completes the family. Also, first two persons of the God-head—the third is the SON.

THREE—Completion—the Trinity.

FOUR—World number—four seasons; points of the compass, etc.

FIVE—Progress, but incompleteness; perfect 3 plus imperfect 2.

SIX—Evil, Satanis.

SEVEN—Dispensational fullness. Divine 3 plus world 4—(seven seals; seven candles, etc.)

EIGHT—New beginnings; resurrection; Jewish circumcision.

NINE—Multiple of THREE.

TEN—Worldly completion. Evil 6 plus world 4.

ELEVEN—Separation; 6 plus 5—Loss; 11 Apostles.

TWELVE—Final completion; gates, tribes, fruits, etc.

THREE

Each of the signs is given with three distinct motions. The grip is given with three distinct movements.

There are three words in each of the passes.

A tree has three divisions—root; trunk; branch; or source; growth; fruitage.

Time has three divisions—present; past; future.

Jesus was persecuted three days.

He had three trials—formal; ecclesiastical; political.

He was tried under three tribunals—Annas; Sanhedrin; the Roman Governor.

Jesus was three times scourged.

Jesus was three times mocked—the robe, the crown, the reed.

There were three sentences—Greek, Hebrew, Latin.

Jesus was crucified on the center of three crosses.

Three classes of people looked on the crucifixion—the mob, the Roman soldiers who crucified him, the gaping multitude.

Three friends looked on his sufferings—the broken-hearted mother; the beloved Disciple; and the trembling Mary.

He left three messages—"Go Ye"; "Teach"; "Baptize."

He lay three days in the tomb.

Three sacred ointments were carried to use on His body —myrrh; alloes; and sacred embalming spices.

His tomb was visited three times—by women; Peter and John; and the Disciples.

He arose the third day.

Three things to give—alms to the needy; comfort to the sad; and appreciation to the worthy.

Since the fall of man there have been three ages, or dispensations. First, the age of God, the Father—from the fall of man to the coming of Christ. At this age, God spoke face to face with man.

The Second age—or the age of God, the Son, was from

the birth of Christ to His ascension, and in this age, God worked through His Son.

The Third age dates from the ascension of Christ to the present time, and in this age, God—the Holy Spirit, rules. It was of this age that Jesus said, "Unless I go, the Comforter cannot come."

The Triangle represents the Trinity. The all-knowing wisdom and the almighty power, and the all-embracing love of God.

There are three distinct lines, or sides, to the Triangle. Without three distinct primary elements there is no life for our being is composed of Body, Mind, and Soul (or Spirit).

There are three great events in a person's life—birth, life and death. Birth is the emerging or coming forth from the unmanifested into a higher plane, or spiritual unfoldment, where experience is gained through suffering and pain, where the soul is refined as gold in a crucible. Life is a battle fought, a battle of the spiritual against the material, self against our lower and animal natures. Death is a transformation, a disintegration of the molecules which years have built up·to our physical bodies and returns them to dust from which they came.

A belief in the Trinity is set forth in the Apostles' Creed of the Thirteenth Century.

FIVE

There are five raps at the door.
There are five points to the Star.
There are five emblematic colors.
There are five emblems and five symbols.
There are five letters in the cabalistic word.
There are five words in the cabalistic motto.

60

There are five signs and five degrees.

Five triangles compose the Pentagon.

There are five divisions to the Eastern Star degrees.

There are five lessons for emulation.

There are five degrees of relationship of women to a Master Mason.

The number five is used in our work twelve times and the number seven, three times; the number three, seven times and many times more as the work progresses.

SEVEN

There are seven ties to the obligation.

Seven officers give instruction.

Seven members constitute a quorum.

Candidates are presented to seven stations in initiation.

The number seven was the most potent number in ancient religions and has deep significance.

The Pythagoreans called seven a perfect number, as it is made up of three and four, two perfect figures—the triangle and the square.

It is a virgin number, because it cannot be multiplied to produce any number within ten, nor can it be produced by multiplication of any number.

The number seven was among the Israelites a symbolic seal of the covenant between God and their nation.

There were seven sentences from the cross.

There were seven candlesticks and seven candles.

The Book has seven seals.

"Seven" assumes in the Bible a great significance, generally indicating completion or perfection.

It is especially prominent in the Hebrew Calendar,

which governed the times of worship and all feasts and fast-ings in the Old Dispensation.

Thus, seven was to be the aggregate number of Holy Convocations of the Hebrew year. (Lev. 23); the seventh day was the Sabbath Day; the seventh week after the Pass-over, was the Sabbath Week; the seventh month, the Sab-bath Month; the seventh year, the Sabbath Year; the great Sab-bath year of Sabbath years, the Jubilee Year.

There are seven weeks between Pentecost and the Pass-over. Seven days were the Priests to be in course of consecra-tion; seven things were offered in sacrifice; seven utensils were to be indispensables of the Tabernacle—the candlestick was to be seven-branched; seven was the number on com-pacts in treaties of peace, in marriage settlements; seven was solemnly emblazoned in the Hebrew oath, the term sig-nifying to "swear," literally meaning to do seven times.

THIRTEEN

Five times does the number 13 occur in the Coat of Arms of the United States.

There are 13 stars, 13 stripes on the shield, 13 arrows in the eagle's claws, 13 leaves on the branch, and 13 letters in *E Pluribus Unum*.

GEMS

ADAH—An Ornament. Integrity
> Gem: *Turquoise*

RUTH—A Friend. Loyalty
> Gem: *Topaz*

ESTHER--A Star. Sparkling Purity. Courage
> Gem: *Diamond*

MARTHA—Instructed by Christ. Fortitude and Abiding Faith
> Gem: *Emerald*

ELECTA—Called of God. Ardor. Zeal. Sacrifice. Hospitality.
> Gem: *Ruby*

FLOWERS

~~~~~~

Flowers are nature's smiles, wrought from her own hues and materials, and are monitors of truth and loving kindness.

They delight the eye, gratify the sense, and are eloquent teachers of purity, humility and love.

Down deep in the shaded valleys, on shaded hillslopes, on mountain crags and on dewy hillsides, along highways, or in cultivated gardens, they greet us with their messages of love and joy.

The foot may crush, the sun may scorch, the flight of seasons cause to wither, they will come again in their loveliness to prove to us the lasting worth of God's love for us in giving the beautiful for our enjoyment.

In the ritual of our Order they assume an important part, suggesting through their forms and colors, fragrance and beauty, the womanly virtues of the five heroines of the Order.

THE VIOLET ☆ *A Symbol of Modesty*
Dedicated to ADAH

The violet is the meekest flower that grows. For its very nature it appeals to us. It is one of the earliest spring flowers, and is found almost every place where perennials grow.

Modest, unassuming, asking only for space to bud and

Flowers

bloom, it thus fulfills its mission. It is the color of the starry-decked heavens. It is obedient to nature, forgetful of snow or sleet, or cold, it comes forth and performs its mission according to God's plan.

It is easy to see why this flower was chosen as a symbol of filial obedience, and it should always remind us that those virtues which were exemplified by Adah should always find a dwelling place in the heart of every member of the Order.

There is a place where only blue violets bloom, and this place is in the heart of all true followers of the plans of God—obedient to His Will and His Love.

THE JESSAMINE ☆ *Loveliness Among the Lowly*
Dedicated to RUTH

This is a midsummer flower and best portrays the humble life of those who walk the paths of loneliness and virtue. Its color is in harmony with the morning glow, the noonday's heat, the sheen of the harvest fields. It harmonizes with all things about it, and creates a beautiful background for God's handiwork, as did Ruth in carrying out God's plan for the continuation of a chosen family. It is a token of patient industry, and its color is an emblem of plenty, reminding us as our pathway is strewn with abundance, we should dispense good cheer and good deeds, never forgetting the necessity of others, or the devotion to principles of right living and truth.

THE LILY ☆ *A Symbol of Peace*
Dedicated to ESTHER

The lily has always been a symbol of the chalice of the world's tears—a cup of morning dew, a home for the beauty

65

and glory of the floral kingdom, and an urn of gladness, of joy and purity.

Tender, beautiful, pure, with its uplifted petals catching the morning fragrance and glory, scattering its wealth of sweetness, even as Esther. A token of light and joy. A symbol of purity, teaching us that pure precepts are usually followed by pure examples, and a pure mind is a generator of pure thoughts. A pure and an upright life can only come from pure thoughts.

The lily is a cultivated flower. Purity often comes from cultivated thoughts . . . and by the practice of the virtue of loveliness we may grow pure in thought and deed.

THE FERN   ☆   *A Symbol of Immortality*
                                                Dedicated to MARTHA

A token of sincerity, and a symbol of faith and immortality. Along mossy banks, across deep marshes, along streams, up on rocky crags and along ledges of strong cliffs and mountains, drop the beautiful waving fronds of the fern. Every place, and any place, where nature has prepared a footing may be found the beautiful fern—emblem of Martha.

It is not a cultivated plant, but grows naturally where it finds a lodging place.

So grows—FAITH in a soil that is ready to receive it. So grows HOPE and BELIEF in the immortality of the soul—planted by God in the heart of everyone—cultivated only by human action, or impulse.

Trees shed their leaves only to be ready to be renewed again with another spring. The evergreen holds its branches high, or pointing downward, all to show that a God of all Good, and a never changing God rules Nature and so, therefore, rules the coming and the going of our own lives. We are

66

born, we live, we die, but death is swallowed up in the victory of a life anew, and as our mortality shall put on immortality, we shall be clothed in Christ's likeness—and live with Him in a life to come. It is not all of death to die nor all of life to live—but a faith that will carry us through is the most assuring, most comforting feeling to have.

THE ROSE ☆ *A Symbol of Love*
Dedicated to ELECTA

Rose means LOVE, deep, enduring love, such as only a mother can give, or a God can show.

The rose is mentioned by the earliest writers of antiquity as an object of culture. Herodotus speaks of the double roses of Jericho, the Solomon Rose of Sharon, and the plantations of roses at Jericho.

The Egyptians valued the rose as they valued their corn. Roses were employed by both Greeks and Romans to decorate their tombs. The rose has been a favorite subject of poets and writers of all countries and ages.

The Greek poets say that the rose was originally white, but was changed to red from the blood of Venus who lacerated her foot with its thorns when rushing to the aid of Adonis.

Many myths and legends attended the rose. The Turks believe the rose sprang from the drops of perspiration of Mahomet, for which reason they will not tread upon a petal of a rose.

The rose was the official seal of Martin Luther. It appeared upon the manuscripts of his Bible, and other items of literature.

Shakespeare makes the rose a division between the house of York and Lancaster.

Solomon valued the rose very highly, and in his songs he

mentions "The Rose of Sharon," which grew on the hills of Judea.

The rose is a token of the final triumph of truth, a symbol of the zeal which should actuate all in their services for truth, and should instill within us that charity which is essential if we receive the reward of the martyr defenders of truth. (Hebrews, Chap. 11. Second Cor., Chapter 13).

COLORS

~~~~~~

COLORS teach the beauty of life.

Colors make a strong appeal to the emotions, even to the emotions of animals.

Color in a broad sense is synonymous with light. If there were no light there would be no color.

The colors of the Eastern Star suggest nothing but the purest thoughts. They are so used as to give further light to the lesson to be taught by the lecture of that particular Point.

The ritual gives a full and complete explanation of the symbolic meaning of these five colors. Together, these colors present a five toned cord of the tie that binds us to the Masonic teachings.

BLUE—consecrated to Jephthah's daughter, takes its color from the cerulean sky under which the mountain maid spent the days of her happy youth, and the vapor tinted mountain tops to which she fled for her two months of consecration before surrendering her life.

This color is also the color of the Holy garment which God commanded Moses to make for Aaron, the High Priest "and he made the robe of the ephod of woven work, all of blue." (Ex. 39:22). This was the garment he must wear when he went before the Lord to pray for the people, a type of the garment of Christ's righteousness, made by His sacrifice for all sinners.

YELLOW—consecrated to Ruth, borrows its golden tint equally from the glaring sun above and the ripened grain below, between which throbbed the faithful heart of that matchless damsel of Moab.

Yellow indicates sincere affection. Gold-yellow means beautiful thoughts, glory, power and action. The gold color is used in the scriptures to symbolize what is divine, pure, precious and useful.

WHITE—consecrated to Esther, suggests the dignity which this heroic green so cheerfully laid aside to preserve God's chosen people from extermination.

It denotes purity, uprightness, conquering faith, and noble qualities of mind and heart. It means chastity, purity, innocence and light.

GREEN—consecrated to Martha, leads the chastened spirit through and beyond the grave to all that is animating, the true thought of a resurrection and a happy reunion with those who have gone before. It is the garb of nature, and thus represents life, because it is associated with springtime. It means immortality of the soul and is symbolic of youth.

It is repeated in nature as it disrobes and again brings forth a renewal of life when springtime comes.

RED—consecrated to Electa, suggests hospitality inculcated in all the teachings of the Order. It suggests warmth, zeal and that fervor that becomes the stimulus for those who practice the Golden Rule.

Because of the association of this color with blood, it has symbolized many attributes of blood. It has signified fire, hatred, cruelty, and passion. It is, symbolically speaking, the life-blood of the Chapter work, as it indicates the fervency and zeal of tried and true servants of God.

THE PENTA COMBINATION

Penta means five

The central star is so placed that the points of red and blue face the East. This combination of color is symbolically arranged. These two colors unite life and executive ability and, placed together in service, their language means "Ruling Power."

The blending of the colors means, symbolically speaking, a blending of the best there is in us, and the unification of all the good in us with those about us to make a complete colorful whole.

No life is lived to itself alone. Whether or not we carry about with us an "aura," or radiate color gleams, there is an undisputed fact that no life is complete within itself. It must be blended in with others, and formed by social contact, and worshipful attitude to our Creator Who gives colors to the universe to break the monotony of scenes, strength to our bodies, enlightenment to our eyes, and intelligence to our countenance.

The primary colors blended in the beautiful rainbow reflect that harmony which should dominate our lives as we mix and mingle with the crowds. Without harmony of thought and action no one is happy or useful.

STATIONS AND OFFICERS

~~~~~~

THESE four Stations compose the "Square" of the Chapter room.

EAST

The East has long been called the source of wisdom, authority and information.

Originally, people worshipped with their eyes towards the East. The sun has its appearance in the East, and this gave rise to the thought that East is the source of all things.

All vegetation, and all humanity, and life, must have the rays of the sun in order to have growth and strength. Hence, East early became the source of life, and to the minds of the Orientals, all power came from the sun. Hence Sun worship, and the many legends from antiquity that may be found in early literature.

The East is occupied by the Presiding Officer, who has control, or authority for instruction and discipline. No one should occupy this station who is not thoroughly capable of presiding without partiality, or prejudice, but will govern with equal justice to all, and use the wisdom and discretion necessary to keep a Chapter in harmony.

Since the East is the source of wisdom, justice and love, so should be the officer who occupies the East in a Chapter.

WEST

The West is the farewell of the sun, the close of life, and the end of time, the farewell of day.

One occupying a seat in the West should see that all members leave the Chapter room in harmony and love. The "farewell" of the meeting should leave an afterglow, as when the sun sets upon a valley in peace. This farewell sweetness should emanate from the officer in the West, who should not fail to make the parting harmonious.

NORTH

Ancient travellers were guided by the North Star. All about them might be darkness and gloom; fears beset them; foes awaited, but the appearance of the North Star dispelled all fear and they were willing to be guided by it at all times.

When a Candidate is "in waiting" she knows not what is before her. She, perhaps, has heard all kinds of ludicrous stories of the manner of initiation but from the moment the officer from the North makes her appearance, she becomes eager to go into the room led by the officer from the North, and as "light" begins to dawn upon her conscience, she more readily appreciates the advice given her in the preparation room. Therefore, the officer from the North should possess many charming virtues that will tend to make the very first impressions lasting and as we desire them to be.

SOUTH

From the South comes the first breath of spring, the fragrance of flowers; the song of birds; the smell of green grass growing; the music of budding trees as life is made anew. Soft zephyrs float out on the perfumed air redolent with life-giving power, and budding nature is awakening with promises of future glory.

So it is becoming in the officer of the South to bring with her a gladness that will keep in motion the hopes kindled by the officer of the North, and to hold this interest throughout the entire ceremony of initiation. This is a most this heroic queen so cheerfully laid aside to preserve God's important office, and when properly filled, one of the most interesting of the entire group.

This officer should radiate gladness, instill confidence, infuse a yearning for light and development in the work of initiation.

First led, as it were, by the North Star into fuller light, the South should lead on to more developed knowledge of the work, never slacking, never allowing for one minute the interest, or attention to waver.

CENTRAL STAR

As the sun's rays, assisted by others of nature's choosing, becomes the germinator of all life, so should the rays of the "Star" become the power through which truths are taught by the lessons of the Star.

Since the Bible is the "Light," or source of wisdom, these lessons should be given in such a manner as to lead to a better development of its full meaning. A mere chanting, or repetition, without interest does not convey the proper meaning. The lesson should be LIVED, and the officer giving her particular part should LIVE while she is giving her lecture, so that the rays of LIGHT from the Altar be not dimmed.

The beautiful color rays as brought out in the lessons

should shine with sparkling beauty, thus focusing upon the central light upon the Altar from which they are all taken.

SOUTH-EAST

The Secretary should be intelligent, alert, accurate, and always reflect the rays of authority which come from the East. Upon her depends much—but she should always remember she is not the chief officer, but is in the East to give out all information that is required of her. Her duties are outlined in the Ritual, and her qualifications should be determined before she is elected as Secretary.

TREASURER

"Keeper of the Treasury," whose duties are outlined in the Ritual. In addition to these, she should bear the confidence of her sisters and brothers and see that all her work is above reproach, safely care for the accounts, and treasury of the Chapter.

ALL OTHER OFFICERS

Whose duties are outlined in the Ritual, and of whose qualifications the Chapter must be the judge.

"Actions speak louder than words" and when an officer is appointed to fill any certain office, it should be the duty of that officer to carry out the instructions of the Matron, and perform the duties of her office with wisdom and discretion.

No task, however small,
Is better done well, than not done at all.

POEMS

~~~~~~

CALVARY'S STREAM IS FLOWING

A crimson stream is flowing from Rugged Calvary,
   A tide of life which cleanses from all impurity;
It is the blood of Jesus, the precious, precious blood,
   By which our souls are ransomed and reconciled to God.

There is a stream of healing, whose waters clear and sweet,
   Are for the weary Nations, helpless at Jesus' feet;
These waters are refreshing, abundant, rich and free, .
   Imparting health eternal and immortality.

O, stream of love eternal! O, source of purity,
   O, grace of God abundant! O, fountain rich and free!
Flow on and flow forever, flow through and through my
     soul,
   With power and with cleansing, till thou hast made me
     whole.

I long for perfect cleansing; I long for perfect peace;
   I yearn to have the conflicts within my spirit cease.
O, stream of life eternal, flow in and make me free
   From all that can defile me, from all impurity.

HOME TOGETHER

The road is rough before our feet,
  The hills are steep and high,
And clouds are gathering overhead
  To shut away the sky.
Perhaps our paths may run apart
  In dark and stormy weather,
But at the nearly evening-time,
  We'll all be home together.

Oh, friend of mine, I grieve to lose
  The grasp of loving hands;
How much we need each other here
  Each fully understands.
But if our pathways meet no more
  In meadow land or heather,
Believe that when the night is come
  We'll all be home together.

So here's a hand that's true, my friend,
  And steadfast, come what may,
God grant our paths run side by side
  And part not all the way.
But if it be that part we must—
  God only knoweth whether—
There's comfort in the thought that night
  Will bring us home together.

THE SIGNET RING

Once in Persia reigned a King,
  Who, upon his signet ring,
Graven a maxim true and wise,
  Which, if held before the eyes,
Gave him counsel at a glance;
  Fit for every change and chance;
Solemn words are they:
  "Even this shall pass away."

Struck with palsy, sere and old,
  Waiting at the gates of Gold
Saith he, with dying breath:
  "Life is done, but what is death?"
Then, in answer to the King,
  Fell a sunbeam on his ring,
Showing by a heavenly ray—
  "Even this shall pass away!"

HOME AT LAST

Hark, the song of holy rapture,
  Hear it break from yonder strand,
Where our friends for us are waiting
  In that golden summer land.
They have reached the port of glory,
  O'er the river they have passed,
And with millions they are shouting
  "Home at last—Home at last!"

Oh, the long and sweet reunion,
  Where the bells of time shall cease,
Oh, the greeting, endless greeting
  On the vernal heights of peace;
Where the hoping and desponding
  Of the weary heart are past,
And we enter life eternal—
  Home at last—Home at last!

Look beyond, the skies are clearing;
  See the mists dissolve away;
Soon our eyes will catch the dawning
  Of a bright celestial day.
Soon the shadows will be lifted
  That around us now are cast,
And rejoicing we shall gather—
  Home at last—Home at last!

THE CROSS

When I survey the wondrous cross
  On which the Prince of Glory died,
My richest gain I count but loss
  And pour contempt on all my pride.

Forbid it, Lord, that I should boast
  Save in the death of Christ, my God.
All the vain things that charm me most,
  I sacrifice them to His blood.

See, from his head, his hands, his feet,
  Sorrow and love flow mingled down,
Did e'er such love and sorrow meet,
  Or thorns compose so rich a crown?

Were the whole realms of nature mine,
  That were a present far too small;
Love, so amazing, so divine,
  Demands my soul, my life, my all.

SUGGESTED QUESTIONS

~~~~~~

ADAH

1—How many judges did Israel have? Which one was the judge spoken of in this lesson?

2—Where was Jephthah when he was chosen Judge of Israel?

3—Had the Temple of Solomon been built at the time of Jephthah?

4—Is the name of "Adah" mentioned in the story of Jephthah's daughter?

5—Why was this name chosen for the Eastern Star?

6—Why did the Jews consider a vow must not be broken?

7—Why should the sword be taken up with the right hand?

8—Which one of the judges was left handed? What event in connection with him is told in the Bible?

9—Why use the veil in this lesson?

10—What are the Emblems? Symbols? Color? Why?

11—Was Adah the only daughter of Jephthah?

12—Why is the "Word" the symbol of this lesson?

13—Why did all Jewish women desire to become a mother?

14—What do you know of "devoted things"?

15—Why was Jephthah placed among the "Roll of Faith" in Hebrew 11?

16—Why is the Open Bible used for this lesson?

17—Who was the last judge of Israel? Who was the first King?

18—Why was Jephthah outstanding among the judges?

19—What do you get from the Pass? The Sign? The Open Bible?

20—What three women of the Bible bore the name of Adah?

21—Do you think God raises up men to carry on His work?

22—Does Adah use the Triangle in her sign? Is this true of all the signs?

23—What does this lesson mean to you?

RUTH

1—In what countries are the scenes of this Star Point laid?

2—Who composed the family of Elimelech?

3—Why did they sojourn in the land of Moab?

4—Why did Naomi want to return to her old home?

5—Why did Ruth decide to accompany Naomi?

6—Quote Ruth's response to Naomi when she was asked to return.

7—How was Naomi received in Bethlehem?

8—Why did she want to be called Mara?

9—Where is this lesson found?

10—What significance as to race had this marriage of Ruth and Boaz?

11—What relation was Ruth's son to King David? Give the name of the son.

12—What other notable event is associated with Bethlehem?

13—Why is this degree called the Widow's Degree?

14—Why is yellow associated with this degree? Why the Sheaf?

15—Who was Boaz? What is the meaning of the word Boaz? (*Strength*)

16—What is the symbol of Ruth? The Emblem of the Second Point?

17—Trace the lineage of Ruth to the birth of Christ.

18—What other Book of the Bible bears the name of a woman?

ESTHER

1—Where may the lesson of this story be found?

2—Where is the scene of this lesson laid?

3—Who was the King mentioned in the time of Esther?

4—Who was Vashti? Why was she dethroned?

5—How came the Jews in Persia at this time?

6—Who was Esther? What was her Jewish name?

7—Who was Mordecai? Haman?

8—Who procured the edict against the Jews?

9—Why had Esther been chosen as Queen?

10—What promise did the King make to Esther?

11—What was the fate of Haman? Who succeeded him?

12—What Jewish feast commemorates the events of this story?

13—Does the name "GOD" appear anywhere in the book of Esther?

14—What is the color of this Point? Why chosen?

15—Why is the Sun appropriate to Esther?

16—What are the Symbols? The Emblems? The Color? Why?

17—Have you read the entire book of Esther?

18—Did you connect Esther with the modern woman of politics?

19—What appeal has this lesson? Why?

20—What do you get from the Sign? (*Appeal to the intelligence, and correct motives in the walk of life*)
21—Tell the story of Esther in your own words.

MARTHA

1—Who composed the family of this story?
2—Where was their home?
3—What do you know about Bethany? What is the meaning of the name?
4—What is the present name of the place?
5—What religious doctrines prevailed at the time of this
Story?
6—Where was Jesus at the time of the death of Lazarus?
7—Why was the story taken from Martha rather than Mary?
8—The shortest verse in the Bible occurs in this story.
What is it?
9—Why is green appropriate to the Star Point? Why evergreen?
10—Why the Broken Column at this Point?
11—What are the Symbols? Emblems? Colors? Floral Emblems?
12—Do you see any significance in the closed grave? The
stone?
13—Was the brother ever seen again after his resurrection?
14—What is this Point intended to teach? Why?
15—What putrid things about us need to be placed in a
closed grave? (*Envy, spite, hatred, malicious speaking,
jealousy*)
16—What things in our nature need to be resurrected? (*Joy,
peace, happiness, love, belief and hope*)
17—Is Martha an example for modern women? Why?
18—Is Mary an example for modern women? Why?

19—Which of the Gospels tell this story? What letters of Paul refer to it?

20—Learn all you can about Bethany—Jerusalem.

ELECTA

1—Where is the lesson of the Fifth Point of the Star found?

2—There were two Saint Johns. Which one wrote the Gospel, 1st and 2nd John? Revelations? Who was the other John?

3—Where did he live a part of his life? Was he one of the Disciples?

4—Who was Electa? Is her name mentioned as such in the Bible?

5—In your opinion, why was the name "Electa" chosen for this Point?

6—Was Christianity officially recognized at that time?

7—Who was the first martyr? Was Electa persecuted?

8—Do you think this lesson should teach us to be firm in our Faith?

9—What is Love? Sacrifice? Faith?

10—What is St. John called? Why? Do you exemplify this in your life?

11—What are the Emblems of Electa? Symbols? Color? Why?

12—Is the double Triangle used in the sign? Why?

13—What does the Cross signify? The Rose? The Color?

14—If Electa represents the Christian Church, does the Rose represent the shed blood of martyrs?

15—What is Zeal? What is Fervency?

16—Why was the Cup chosen for this Point? Is the symbol of the Cup always suffering? Joy? Does it mean "Fate"?

17—Should we share our Cup of Joy, of Sorrow, of Gladness, with our fellow-beings?

18—Was Jesus called the "Rose of Sharon"?

19—Was He called the "Word"? Was He called the "Lily of the Valley"? Was He called the "Sun of Righteousness"? Was He called "The Lamb slain for the Sins of the world"? Was He called "The Lion of the Tribe of Judah"?

Where are these symbols found?

What is a pentagon? Square? Triangle? Circle?

Who are the Electas of today? What was the commandment of John?

Which is the Daughter's Degree? Which is the Widow's? The Wife's? The Sister's? The Mother's?

Do Masons obligate themselves to take care of these members of the household?

Question—Many times have we been asked, "Why should one never pass between the Altar and the East when the Chapter is at labor?"

Answer—In practically all religious ceremonies it would be considered highly improper for a worshiper to pass between the altar and the priest who was officiating at the altar. In a symbolic scene the Worthy Matron while engaged upon the work of the Chapter from her station in the East is officiating at the altar of Freemasonry. Therefore, no one should pass between her and that which symbolizes this altar except in performance of ritualistic work which is a part of the service itself. It is an unwritten law of Masonry not to pass between the altar and the East.

Question—Should the Bible be open on the Altar during public installation?

Answer—At public installation the Chapter is at rest; therefore, the Bible is not displayed on the Altar, unless properly provided for in your By-laws.

Question—When should officers vacate their stations and step down on the floor in the closing ceremony?

Answer—Not until after the Matron has declared the Chapter closed and gives the final knock with her gavel. Until that moment the Chapter is at labor and the stations should be occupied.

Question—Is it necessary to hold one patriotic meeting each year?

Answer—You are being protected by your Government. Show your appreciation to that Government by actions as well as by words.